175

Woodpeckers

poems

Shiv K. Kumar

Sidgwick & Jackson
London

First published in Great Britain in 1979
by Sidgwick & Jackson Limited

Grateful acknowledgement is made to the editors of the follow-
ing periodicals and anthologies in which several of these poems
had their first appearance:
*Hemisphere, The Greenfield Review, The New Quarterly, The
New Quest, The Illustrated Weekly of India, The Hindustan Times,
Debonair, Indian Verse, International Poetry Review* and *The
Journal of Indian Writing in English.*
Oxford University Press is thanked for permission to reprint
certain sections of 'Broken Columns' from *Subterfuges.*

ISBN 0 283 98486 4 (hard)
ISBN 0 283 98487 2 (paper)

Printed in Great Britain by
Latimer Trend & Company Ltd Plymouth
for Sidgwick & Jackson Limited
1 Tavistock Chambers, Bloomsbury Way
London WC1A 2SG

Contents

Broken Columns	1
Flower-pot in my Study	18
Crematorium in Adikmet, Hyderabad	19
Mango Grove	20
The Taj	21
My Son	22
At the Ghats of Banaras	24
School Children During Lunch Break	25
An Old Dry Well	26
At the Customs Counter	27
To an Unborn Child	28
Insomnia	29
Young Maidservant	30
My Aunt	31
To a Prostitute	32
Love Letter	33
Rain	34
Thanksgiving	35
A Dead Bird on an Electric Pole	36
A Pregnant Woman in the Queue	37
My Right Hand	38
Midnight Musings	39
Lord Venkateswara's Temple	40
Detachment	42
Autumn	43

For
Reg Foakes

Broken Columns

'You're now four;
you may drink up
all the glaciers
nibble at raw pebbles
but not suck away.'

Father's barb fell blunted
against Mother's smile.
A hairbreadth guilt ran
down the wall's spine.

I slammed my *Songs the Letters Sing*
at page nine:
   'Krishna is on the swing
   Let him sing to Mother.'

I plunged into precocity.

II

I am seven.
Father walks me down to Rosary Convent School
beyond the butcher's.
Heads, intestines, thighs and shoulders—
scraped wounds awaiting dressing—
hang by invisible hooks.
Behind the counter looms
the assassin chopping off
life into fragments.
Father explodes:

> 'Karma will run its cycle when these
> maimed animals rise
> to gobble down these shoppers.'

We jump across the pavement
to encounter a beggar's sunken belly—
the map of India
in Mercator's projection.

III

At ten I play hide and seek
down the school-lane in a shop
stacked with teak and deodar
and suddenly Sheila's chequered
skirt blows into life.
All the mynas on its border
flutter out of the pattern.
I transfix her behind a pillar
of deodar and my lips
release the tongue to plumb
the Bay of Bengal.

Is there a point at which
even parallel lines meet
out of sheer exhaustion?

IV

At dusk Father shuffles us all
about on the coir-mat to pray.
We spout chants from the *Gita*:
'Feed not thy desire
on objects of sense.
But like a tortoise
folding up its limbs within the shell
withdraw into supreme wisdom.'

A puff of deodar rustles
through a girl's skirt
and two tender legs
gyrate the air into fuzzy yearnings.

V

At fourteen the Mughal Empire
crumbles in a battered class-room.
  'When gold rusts
  what can iron do?'
The teacher blares against
a parched sky: sweat drips
from all the cornices.
   'It wasn't the British might
   but our own degeneracy. . . .'

A lizard creeps on its
chromium-plated belly
to the blackboard's edge
flashing its tongue.
Thirst lashes our palates
but we lie still
under the Empire's debris.

Instantly the teacher pulls out his
flask to swig down his butter-milk.
Little boulders of fluffy cream
assault his black moustache.
Across a sedate nose
two bespectacled eyes glow
at visions of green regeneration.
We pant on the dunes
of the relentless Sahara.

VI

At twenty
I see a girl's bodice shimmer
in the water's eye. I am
the Adam who has just founded
a new city
named all its streets.

The blood sang in the tree's veins
as I wedged into the trunk.
Somewhere below the roots
stone melts into water
and silence is no virtue.
No commitment to the stars, she knew,
only a beetle's mating drone.

Yet the first-born
sometimes cries in the autumn evenings
for that little island in the sun
round which cluster fledgelings
after the summer rain
to splash about
in mysteries.

VII

Father sniffs danger in scraps
of scented pink paper
blown from my pockets.
Subterfuges can cloak only the turret
not the stereobate anchored in certitude.
>   'And no blinkers can hoodwink
>   the albino glow in your third eye.
>   Better seek the temple priest
>   before hunger ruptures your soul.'

In the meditation-room
of the Siva temple
the high-priest communes with Brahma.
Wrapped in saffron loin-cloth
he lets his long, grey hair
cascade down to life's quiddity.
As he beckons me into the dark chamber
I pull myself out of the earth's orbit
into blank space.
>   'An obedient child you are.
>   Your father has told me all.'

A cold jasmine-braceleted hand
caresses my nape;
my nerves tingle like a horse's flanks
on a frigid morning.

'Self-control is the force
that keeps the sky's circus-tent
staid above the multitude.
Remember, my son,
where a woman's body creases
at the core of existence
a sewer runs through the dark
foliage. There's the wound
that abjures the herb,
outstares the sun into surrender
till down the gorge we sink
into oblivion.'

But as I emerge from the netherworld
an aroma of deodar wells up
and a cluster of mynas hurls
defiance at the truth.

VIII

The P & O Liner bellows
into the Ballard pier
sucks in a swarthy cargo from Bombay
then breaks into a nervous whirr.
The whales and sharks join in
on this random pilgrimage to an alien land.

Under the lapis lazuli Cambridge sky
the languid pavements dream
of Ogden and Wittgenstein.
Near the Mill Lane pub,
spilling over with bitters
and blasphemies, the suave
Cam changes horses.
The punts glide down to
a new Utopia.

My tutor, a retired missionary
from Agra, digs his webbed hands
into my tropical past
but the Cam is no Ganges
nor do the piebald ducks
meditate on Brahma.

Beyond the campus precincts
argent bulls chase mottled butterflies
into the livid horizon.
Freedom bares its sallow fangs
for the primal assault.

Susan's chestnut hair touches off
a forest fire trapping
all the sparrows in a single tree.
Her beefed tongue freshens up
all profanities.

Young Siddhartha swigs off
the champagned nipples
(time to quaff all the glaciers!)
and kneels before the fount
for redemption.

As for penance, he consigns to
Byron's Pool all his brown idols
(multi-limbed like giant wasps)
manacled with his sacred thread:
gods like wily seducers
goddesses, with phoney breasts and thighs,
incarnating Mother India.

The letter home to Mother
still breathes nostalgia:
   'Do the mauve bougainvillias
   over the rear gate still bite
   into the Ashoka tree?
   And I pray your coconut-water
   offerings to the Hanuman Temple
   will lubricate Father's gout.'

But Karma closes in fast—
Susan surf-rides to the other
bank of the Jordan
for fresh strawberries.

The sunken gods wail
from the Pool's abysm:
        'Freedom is the demon
            that devours its own brood.'

IX

Dry grass sings
in the Ely churchyard.
Two fugitives from Trinity and Girton
kneel beneath a discreet mulberry tree
to brew cabalas.
The dead, their mouths gagged
with brown earth, groan
under the weight of shadows.

The eye sees no turnstile
when its ligaments burn
and so we dragged the stars
into the ritual.

Two gates to purgatory—
her toy mouth that gets drunk
on water and her silk-knotted navel
deepening into the dark ingress.

The creepers on the wall
have no clear concept of truth.
If fed on cactus-milk they
may grow into pythons
to stifle the church.

Her eye has not yet returned
from the steeple.
I'll wait on the plains
for the dragonfly to land.

Far away
Cambridge is summoning
all its dead
for a fresh burial.

X

I fly back to my roost
over the Gateway to India.

The bird that stretches its wing
beyond the water's brink
often lands on some insidious rock.
Even the sky has its enemies—
the ungroomed pine, the choleric air
the hybrid moon.

I sit on the festooned dais
beside a woman I had only half known.
Seven circles round the holy fire
incensed by rice, turmeric and camphor.
As the high priest, squatting in his
albescent dhoti (his pouch sizzling
in greasy sweat), shuffles on his cushioned
haunches, two sagging testicles peer through.
Briskly he camouflages the primal nodes
like a dog covering up his shit.
> 'And now you may bring forth
> children, not creatures of lust
> but servants unto the Lord.
> Shantih!'

It's done—
the word becomes flesh
the prophet may now walk on water.

I look at my bride's crabbed fingers
closing into a fist.

XI

I carry my bride home—
a fungal seed to breed hydras.

The first sunrise leaves at my door
a dead cockroach
in the milk-bottle,
news of the porcupine's resurrection
and a defaced horoscope.

Where was Leo when Scorpion crawled
into his den to spray
virus on the damp walls?
While she dreams of the hawk's talons
clutching at the bird,
I clasp the bedstead
like a woman in labour pains.

Think cool—
think of the ecru oysters
drinking green bubbles—
the resurgent snail carrying stoically
its burden of darkness.

But when the pines drown
the wind's baritone and
the word loses its potency
nothing but the slow grind
towards the primeval umbra.

XII

Your eye was clear
like the old gypsy's crystal,
your hand steady on the skipping rope.
That was not the moment for you
to comprehend the meaning
of meaning.
How could a zebra be yoked to carry
cabbages to the market-place?

Contradictions filled the air:
worms eating the fish
a midget hacking away at the oak
the mirror smudging the face.

That fateful night
your mother's last avalanche—
and the wan cymbals of the moon
striking up spectral music.
The cobra eye held me
whichever way I turned;
venom oozed from the earth
to blight all roots.

My clairvoyance prompted me to action.
I bolted, scaled a high rampart to flee
abandoning you to the enemy.
But I loved you most when I forsook you.

In anger, once, I even doubted your genesis
(which one of your mother's men?)
but my father's portrait peered
from the mantlepiece, its contours
merged into yours, ring upon ring,
and I cursed myself for the sacrilege.

Last night I dreamt I saw
on a beige boulder, a tiny bird
the same colour as your skirt—
shaking the hairpin off
its incipient downy feathers—
its beady eyes bulged with desire.
And then another young bird—
some flurried initiation
into the new metaphysic and the clouds
bore them away above highlands and rivers
to a country where the mother-hen
doesn't cackle away
the doors don't slam
and your bed is your own.

Flower-pot in my Study

Stirrings in a painted skull.
Its remotest fears have come true—
procreation is for the living only.
At best one can prolong life
on visions of raindrops on the sill.

To its asthmatic leaves and stems
breathing the hallowed air
of hardbound Plato and Kant,
all seasons are the same.

Like a teddy-bear's button-eyes
its berries dazzle
with their precocious stare.

Dappled birds that sometimes bounce in
through the window
sing of a sunburnt slave who once
carried a princess away.

Dark silence—
compulsion to smoulder
and commitment to unveil beauty
to the master alone.

Crematorium in Adikmet, Hyderabad

Incessant din of beggars
and chants.
A skull rolls out of a drainhole.

Perched on the wall a vulture cogitates
upon human avidity—flesh offered
to the flames, bones and ashes
to the Ganges. No leavings
for the living.

Inside the courtyard six bare platforms
of brown earth turned ashen grey
under centuries of fires fed on
cinnamon, camphor and butter.

Here the earth replenishes itself—
wipes out a name to welcome
a fresh arrival.

And now my father's head
awaits my hand.
The world crackles into a bonfire.
The priest chants louder for a generous tip.

Mango Grove

Above my head clusters of virgin breasts
of peasant women
kneeling over graves
for boons.

The white sun hurls its red
shafts through the sparse leaves
to singe my left toe.
I assume another stance
to dodge the inevitable.

A snake doodles its neutral course
along a dry bed of cacti.

The wind that soughs through this maze
has no assonance—
only the rasp of an alligator's
tail lashing the sand.

This summer may never end.

The Taj

Since this dream had a sharper edge
he engraved it before dawn
in marble (whiter than a nun's veil)
lest its sequence drown
in the muezzin's call.

Under moonlight, a pair
of shaggy dogs caught
in a hot clasp behind the rear minaret.
No emperor's law now prohibits
love's parody.

Fissures in its rectum—
now a renovator's nightmare.
How long can it withstand
the riverbed's lethal teeth?

My Son

Now hear me first
before you claim
your share of the booty.

That night I fought on another front
for other causes
and you were not even a speck
on my cognition's periphery.

Like a rhino
gored in the groin
I charged into my woman
nuzzling my head
into her supple breasts
like a young calf—
sucked blood from her navel

till the oyster's silver gullet
opened out to receive the drop.
Then I slumped beside the torso
deflated
limp-eyed with a dead-bird's stare.

Were you with us even then
like the third traveller
on the road to Emmaus—
seeing, hearing everything?

After nine harvest moons
one afternoon
you barged in knocking the front
door off its hinges
to grab my woman
nibble toothlessly at her moist nipples.

Even impostors have some graces
but you arrive with the assurance
of a state warrant
and I surrender willingly
to you—
my compeer.

At the Ghats of Banaras

Between its carrion teeth
the Ganges can hold three live fishes—
fins, bones, and eyes.

A child's lissom body
in a jute bag;
the warm ashes of a young courtesan;
and once I saw a man ferry across
on a sleazy raft to drop
his pet dog and bless
the sharks that carried the prize away.

A priest's chant
tender but peremptory
churns the viscid waters
into submission.

On the western ghat
a glassy-eyed crocodile dips
into the sacrosanct waters
to cleanse its scales—
its belly mirroring
all faces of death.

School Children During Lunch Break

At noon the dam collapses—
the waters swish and swerve.

Freedom leaves scars
on the knee, elbow
and heart.

A flower-bed lies trampled—
a squirrel shoots up the swing
to caper in the air.

And then the siren's call—
terror to the fugitives.

The coffin clenches its teeth
though beneath its lid the grasshopper
is still poised for a curvet.

The sky drops pollens
over the dead.
The earth smooths its creases.

The wind no longer sings.

An Old Dry Well

A rundle of the sky
lies buried here.
It's not the first time the red
granite has cracked up to let
a bush grow between its abscessed teeth.

The snakes breed in dark
crevices under maimed spouts
syllabling some ancient dialect.

Years ago
a prince reined in his stallion here
to fill up his wineskin.
And then a whole battalion
ravished it
under the scorched sky.

Resilience is not for everybody—
some perish in the womb
before sunrise.

At the Customs Counter

The sinister eye has chosen me
for desecration.
The hooked beak pecks
into my nascent guilt.

Dismembered kidneys, tendons
and lungs quiver on the postmortem
table in mute vulnerability.

Like a blue-blooded virgin raped
by a larrikin, I totter
on the pavement—
a limber corpse slung across my shoulders
hurling imprecations.

To an Unborn Child

It matters little whether you dismount
from lightning's warhead
or a grizzled cloud's belly
you'll land only on this uncarpeted
reef whence tired seagulls
read prophecies in the water's sunglass.

I'm sorry you'll inherit
this subfusc earth.
We've just moved into this limbo
whose walls are papered with unpaid bills.
And on each day of reckoning
I play truant while your mother
feigns hysteria.

Come on in—
we're waiting.

Insomnia

My wife snores. My son's dream
fingers have reached the sideboard's
top-shelf for Cadbury.
The sky grins through a handful
of stars while I hold the defiant
pills in my torpid hand.

I'm a double agent. I'll drug
my watch dog to burgle my own house.
I know where my wife's secrets
lie sealed. Each night I hear
the same tattoo in my skull's chamber.

I have counted all the stars
over my terrace. The steel bars in my
neighbour's balcony are twenty one
and three suburban freight trains rumble past
the rail-crossing between two and four.

Darkness now snaps at the seams.
A hymn floats across the sky
like a bird's warble.

And somewhere down the lane a hand-pump
creaks—the milkman's bottle
jingles at my doorstep.

I must walk through the day's fire
to let another moon demolish me.

Young Maidservant

Still there is one day more
to live
before the tadpoles wallop
limpid waters into slush again.

Three times a week
ardent fingers furbish up
my dead soul
ferret wasps out of
my crinkled bed.

A mere smile can be a ritual
and a frank swivel of the hips
send gazelles capering
through infinite space.

Is it then some double vision?
To knead the dough of wedlock
on sullen evenings
when nobody calls—or
look forward to the other moon
only three constellations away
and feel the tenderness
of larks.

My Aunt

A spinstered bundle of eroded bones
rocks in a deck chair.
Puffs away at a silver-muzzled
hubble-bubble—
the same hooked nose as my father's.
Her hair like sparse Bermuda grass—
her breasts two sagging balloons.

The dull eye, is not
cataract's legacy but
a keyhole through
which she views on the radar
a black-moustached youngman
who once took her
to drink with all other beasts
at the only pool in a dark forest.

Now she smoulders in nicotine
till the smoke-screen will smother
all the stars.

To a Prostitute

I have come to join
the congregation
wash my hands at the same font
where others have dropped their fingers
and walked away.

On your forspent thighs
juvenile tourists who had
only a glimpse of
the inner shrine
have left rude etchings
of name, place and time

which, in fact, never change,
for my son will ferment
the same yeast
as my father's father
and what you offer me now
was also my mother's gift
to a stranger.

My wife awaits me round the corner
to reclaim what's left of me.

Love Letter

The words squirm
like bloated scorpions.
A grotesque dwarf is drinking
from my cup.

No exit now.

A mere scrap of paper
can be one's undoing.
I wonder who this woman is.
Signs herself off with a pair
of rouged lips.
And he somnambulates at noon
from room to room
cursing God for his monism.

What's it that one woman has
and the other hasn't?

With me he's now civil—
only stares
with basilisk eyes.

Rain

Lightning's weals on the
sky's lavendered back
for adultery.
The cloud's swollen eye bursts
into the surgeon's pan.

A silhouetted tree
rolls up its bottoms
to escape the Flood.

I never broke any law
of the god's stern eye.
Yet this fulvous moisture
on my palm
my body drenched in cold sweat—
in pain.

Thanksgiving

In flamboyant regalia
the turkey struts about
on legs of ribbed steel.
A tiara'd head juts into
the dungheap for jades.
A hen with five chicks
trails behind for cover.

Then the cook's hatchet
got him in the backyard—
his crimson blood might have served
my fragile aunt
for transfusion.

Now he lies dressed up on table
in front of Picasso's 'Fruit Bowl'—
a Gulliver besieged by knives and forks
while we offer supplication to the Lord.

All prayer is dual.
What was his last wish?

A Dead Bird on an Electric Pole

A stringless kite caught
in the bare twigs
gasps in the flushed air
seething with worms.

The invisible always hurts more.

The flint eye goggles
at the iron earth.
The open beak dangles from the noose—
its clipped shadow leaps across horizons.

The dead gape eternally
if they don't seal their mouths
at the pain's fatal stroke.

The electric chair is neutral
to bird, assassin and saint.

Around the scaffold a thrush
is looping the loop—
its throat jammed in a mute requiem.

A Pregnant Woman in the Queue

Subtly the grocer balances
paradoxes
on the Ptolemic axis—basmati
rice against dead weights.

The queue stands frozen
like an old snake in snow.
Only an oblique glance
probes this woman
robed in languor.

One may consolidate the gains discreetly
or share the night's secret in the market-place.
The searchlight illuminates
the river's womb whence
the starfish will soon
leap into light.

The man who ploughed the meek
earth perhaps never returned
during the lean season.

How much can you carry
on your petite feet?
You may move up, Ma'am,
I can wait.

My Right Hand

has just come home
after its last hunt
gashed with crisscrosses.

If nothing ever dies
this concave palm
is a granary of memories—
taut nipples that pricked up
their ears at the wind's caress.

The silver mackerel
has slithered through my fingers
that will never again curl round
the dove's breast
nor grope in bed
for the sundered breath.

The whole town is mourning
the dead—the hand in its lithic
tomb guarded by the black angel
with a sardonic smile.

Midnight Musings

Ether-soaked thoughts rise
on arthritic knees.
Black coffee
a slice of the white monk's bread
the cat's eerie purr.

Any woman can get me now.

The moment of despair
has no age
no discretion.
At fifty-two I see eucalyptus
thighs waiting to be hustled
by a mere sunset.

Lord Venkateswara's Temple

A sinuous ant-line of bare feet
stone eyes
trudges up a monolithic rock
to a distant vision.

The same route as my ancestors took
to affirmation
and denial.

Here the divine munificence is boundless—
a devoted ruler's elephant was once blessed
with a litter of nine—
all male.

Oppressed by omniscience
the Lord smiles at daily somersaults—
why should repentance endure
beyond sunset?

Once, so goes the legend,
a young fisherwoman in rags
came to the Lord straight
from her son's burial—
lay prostrate at the shrine's threshold
but asked for no boon
not even peace for her son's soul.

Just then the temple's golden cupola
reeled, the Lord's bejewelled arm
rose in benediction and He smiled

while the high priest surveyed
the woman's flanks—
the length of a cushioned bed.

Detachment

Between the lean man's
tears over a mud grave
pockmarked with the rain's spittle

and the stray donkey
shaking off
the dog's barking
with a quiet shrug

I have faltered
between two truths.

Let the waters carry away the ashes
swiftly past the antique bridge
not swing back to smudge
the rock that has known many a corpse.

Autumn

Here in the open privacy
of a borrowed room
we may talk only in luteous
syllables that drop furtively
on the vacuous promenade
beyond the deadman's pool.

I rise from my bed
in search of movement
in the grass
but nothing stirs
not even my wife deserting.

Shiv K. Kumar

Poet, playwright, short-story writer and critic, Shiv K. Kumar has published three volumes of verse (*Articulate Silences, Cobwebs in the Sun* and *Subterfuges*); a play (*The Last Wedding Anniversary*); several short stories (some of which have been broadcast in the World Service of the BBC); and literary criticism (including *Bergson & the Stream of Consciousness Novel*).

Kumar holds a Ph.D. in English literature from Cambridge, and in 1978 he was elected a Fellow of the Royal Society of Literature. He has lectured in the U.K., the States and Australia—as Commonwealth Visiting Professor of English at the University of Kent (Canterbury), Distinguished Professor of English at the University of Northern Iowa, and Cultural Award Visitor in Australia. He is at present Chairman, Department of English and Dean of the School of Humanities at the University of Hyderabad.